About the Book

In this book we travel through the second largest country in the world, a country still not fully explored which contains the world's oldest and some of its youngest mountains and is a treasure chest of mineral wealth unlike any other land.

We learn its geography from the Arctic to the borders of the United States, from the coastal peaks along the Pacific Ocean across the wheat-producing prairies to the fishing provinces of the Atlantic. In our travels we meet people who have come to settle there from China, Czechoslovakia, the Soviet Ukraine, and a dozen other nations. We visit an Eskimo town, admire the skill of Indian cowboys, and learn what the government is doing to help these Canadians make progress in modern ways of living. We follow the trails of French explorers in picturesque Quebec and meet modern explorers who live on floating ice packs in the Arctic Ocean.

We find of special interest projects, past and present, built or planned by the United States and Canada together. These include the St. Lawrence Seaway, the DEW line, the damming of the Columbia River, and the harnessing the tides of the Bay of Fundy for the production of electric power.

We discover how individual our hosts are, with the various provinces and nationality groups preserving their own customs and even languages, and the problems the national government faces as it tries to unite its peoples and regions.

We spend a wonderful few days with one of Canada's many engineering families, families on the move, from dam to mine to power plant, as the country opens up its resources. In the wilderness surrounding the construction camp, we fish and ride and hunt, keeping an eye out to avoid the cougars.

When we say good-bye, it is with the glad knowledge that we are welcome to return any time, without passports, across a border which has remained unguarded for more than 100 years.

About the Illustrator

MARVIN BESUNDER is a portrait painter, as well as an illustrator. He has a degree from New York University and has studied at the Art Students League. Mr. Besunder has illustrated several other books for children. He lives in Forest Hills with his Canadian wife and their two children.

About the Author

FRANCES ROLLINS has explored some of Canada's remotest regions by jeep, horse-back, helicopter, and fishing trawler and on foot. She has lived on location with construction camp families in the wilderness, followed the Columbia River to its source, climbed glaciers, and slept on pine boughs. Her Canadian friends include Gaspé fishermen, old-timers with gold-rush stories, young engineers and their chil-dren, and Eskimo artists.

Her home is full of Canadian treasures; totem poles, hand-woven baskets, berry-dyed linens, wood carving from Quebec, and jade from British Columbia.

The author of several children's books on foreign lands, she has served with many organizations interested in youth or international relations, or both, most recently with the Experiment in International Living.

About the GETTING TO KNOW *Series*

This round-the-world Series not only covers everyday life in many countries and regions, including their geography and history, but also highlights *what's new today.* The Series offers timely — and often first — reports on the birth of new nations in Africa and Asia, splitting of ancient nations like China, the let's-get-together movement of members of Europe's and Latin America's common markets, and the struggle of two-thirds of the world to attain the good life possessed by the other third. *To keep each book up to date in these fast-changing times, it is revised with every new printing.*

Specific countries in the *Getting to Know* Series are determined by a survey of curriculum specialists in the fifty states. Made every two years, the survey is used to relate G.T.K. subject matter to classroom needs. To insure intimacy, as well as im-mediacy, authors are chosen first of all for the quality of their personal experience with the subject matter. All *Getting to Knows* are also checked by experts prior to publication.

Getting to Know

CANADA

by FRANCES ROLLINS

illustrated by MARVIN BESUNDER

COWARD-McCANN, Inc.   NEW YORK

*For our friends of Sainte Rose,
Gaston and Louise Tremblay*

Library of Congress Catalog Card Number: AC 66-10938

Editor of this series: Sabra Holbrook

PRINTED IN THE UNITED STATES OF AMERICA

Some say Canada's name came from the Indians. *Kanata* in Iroquois means a collection of cabins, and long ago, that's all Canada was. There's also a legend that Spanish pirates once set foot on its bleak northeastern coast and cried *"Acá nada"* — nothing of value here.

Like most legends, the *Acá nada* story is more romantic than truthful. Even the earliest explorers saw the riches of this upper half of the North American continent. Today, equipped with new knowledge, modern tools and restless imagination, Canadians are continuing to explore the wealth with which nature has blessed their land. They are drilling deep into their mountains and valleys, down beneath ice and snow, under the glacial crust of thousands of years. They are forcing their rivers, prairies, forests and coastal seas to yield treasure that would dazzle a pirate's eye.

7

This treasure chest, Canada, is the second largest country in the world after the Soviet Union. The lower edge of the chest rests on the states of Maine, New Hampshire, Vermont, New York, Minnesota, North Dakota, Montana, Idaho and Washington. In the southeast, Canada and the United States share the Great Lakes except Lake Michigan, which is entirely in the United States. Where the top of the North American continent breaks up into islands surrounded by the Arctic Ocean, Canada reaches to the North Pole. She borders Alaska in the northwest, and stretches from the Pacific Ocean to the Atlantic. In the northeast, Baffin Bay and Davis Strait separate her from Greenland.

East and west, mountain ranges rise from the coasts. The Appalachians continue from the United States into eastern Canada. Here too are the Laurentians, the world's oldest mountains, their summits flattened by the weight of the glacial ice that once covered them. In the west are some of the world's youngest mountains, the Coastal Range, also the sharp-peaked Rockies, the purple Cascades, the reddish Selkirks and other smaller chains.

Central Canada is fertile prairies in the south. In the north is the Laurentian Plateau, or Canadian shield, a rocky, forested, sparsely inhabited land of many lakes. Farthest north is the frozen Arctic.

From sea to sea, from the Arctic to the United States, Canada is divided into ten provinces. Partly coastal land and partly island, the province of Newfoundland, famed for its fishing banks, lies farthest

east. The mainland section of Newfoundland is called Labrador. Newfoundland is one of the foggy Atlantic provinces. South of it are the others: New Brunswick, Prince Edward Island and Nova Scotia. They were settled mainly by the French and Scotch (Nova Scotia means New Scotland) and by people from the thirteen American colonies who were loyal to the British king during our revolution for independence. West of Labrador is Quebec, once the

9

stronghold of France in the New World. Next to Quebec is industrial Ontario and beyond lies Canada's breadbasket, the wheat-growing prairie provinces of Manitoba, Saskatchewan and Alberta. In the north and west Alberta begins to rise to the mountains that cover the Pacific province of British Columbia.

In the far north are two territories, the Yukon, once famed for gold, and the Northwest Territories, which include the Arctic. Today the northern territories, not yet wholly explored, are a mixture of old and new. The fur trapper still hunts by canoe, while atomic submarines glide under the polar ice.

In these provinces and territories live some 20 million people, 70 percent of them in cities, especially the cities in Quebec and Ontario. Their ancestors, sometimes their parents or they themselves, have come not only from England, Scotland and France, but from Japan, China, Germany, the Soviet Ukraine, Italy, the Netherlands, the Scandinavian countries, Czechoslovakia, Poland and Portugal. Canada has many Indians, too, and in the north, Eskimos.

These groups like to keep their own customs, even their own languages. There is a story about a German boy working on a dam in British Columbia. He and his fellow workers spoke only German. One day he told his boss, who spoke both German and English, that he wanted a better job in a nearby aluminum smelter. "You will have to learn English then," the boss said. The German boy got himself a job with a group of foresters whom he supposed to be English speaking. After a few months he came back to his boss and boasted that he could speak English. "Let's hear you," replied the boss. The boy chattered in Portuguese. The foresters had been Portuguese, not English.

The French of Quebec, especially, cling to their language and their ways. In deference to them, French is an official language of the country, along with English. So conscious of their different ways of life are Quebec and British Columbia at the eastern and western boundaries of the nation that they have exchange visits for students — the kind of program usually arranged only between separate countries!

Nor are language and custom the only differences among Canadians. The different provinces are extremely jealous of their political rights. When the United States and Canada agreed on a treaty for joint development of the Columbia River, which flows from British Columbia to the state of Washington, Canada had to get approval from its own province of British Columbia before the treaty could be signed!

The power of the provinces and the individuality of groups from other lands make it difficult for the Canadian government to unify the vast country. The Prime Minister, who is the chief executive, is sometimes jokingly called "Prime Minister of all the Canadas." The government is trying to change the Constitution so that there will be a clearer set of rules for the powers of the national government.

The Prime Minister is the leader of the political party with the greatest number of members in the Canadian Parliament. The Parliament has two houses. Members of the Senate are chosen by the Prime Minister and his cabinet and remain in office until they are seventy-five. Members of the House of Commons are elected for five-year terms by the people. There are also strong provincial legislatures and a Premier for each province.

The government is called a confederation. It was formed in 1867, when the British, who ruled Canada then, approved the efforts of some of the provinces to get together for their mutual benefit. The provinces established a common government, copied mostly from the British but also partly from the U.S. A Governor-General still represents the British Monarch but, since 1931, neither the Monarch nor the Governor has had any real power. In that year Canada became independent and joined the British Commonwealth, an association of former colonies and dominions. Canada is also an important member of the United Nations and the North Atlantic Treaty Organization (NATO), an association of North American and Western European countries.

13

NEW

OLD

Canada feels close to the United States and to Britain, but the majority of Canadians are never more wholeheartedly Canadian — despite their differences — than when someone suggests they should strengthen their ties with either country. Their flag, which once resembled the British flag, was changed in 1965. The new flag bears a Canadian national emblem — a red maple leaf — on a white field, with vertical red bars at either end.

The nearly 4,000-mile-long border between Canada and the United States has been unguarded for more than 100 years and the citizens of both countries can cross it at will without passports. Canada sells more than half her exports to the United States and buys almost 70 percent of her imports from us. Canadian-made automobiles can be bought in the United States and our automobiles can be sold in Canada without tariffs, the taxes usually charged on international sales. Some Canadians, looking at such facts, feel it would be an advantage for Canada and the United States to become one country. "One continent, one nation," they say. But this slogan angers other Canadians. They prefer to stay independent.

The beginnings of Canada were bloody. The land was the scene of a great struggle between the British and the French. Later there were conflicts between the United States and Canada over boundaries. Because we live together on one continent, our history is tied up with Canada's in many ways. Among the explorers who opened up our Mississippi River were three who set out from French Canada — La Salle, Marquette and Jolliet.

The earliest explorer to set foot there was probably Leif Ericson, in the year 1000. Then came the Englishman John Cabot in 1497

and in 1534 the Frenchman, Jacques Cartier. The first settlement was established by another Frenchman, Samuel de Champlain, in 1608. Champlain also explored the Great Lakes, the St. Lawrence River, and the coastline south to what became Massachusetts. He charted the rivers in territory which is now the state of Maine and discovered Lake Champlain in what is now northern New York. By the middle of the 17th century, New France, as Canada was then called, was governed as a French colony.

French explorers like Cadillac, who founded Detroit, where Cadillac automobiles are made today, and Duluth, who explored Lake Superior and founded the city of Duluth, Minnesota, began opening the colony's west. With them came the *coureurs des bois,* French fur trappers, most of whom were really fur smugglers. They hunted and sold without licenses, living in the woods with Indians. They, too, helped to map the sprawling new land.

The English, meanwhile, weren't idle. Their trappers were organized as the Hudson's Bay Company in 1670 and a race for control of the fur trade and conquest of half a continent was on.

The French, aided by Huron Indians, attacked British colonies in New England. The British, aided by Iroquois Indians and New Englanders, conquered the French province of Acadia in 1710 and changed its name to Nova Scotia. Scotchmen came to settle there and the Acadians were exiled to British colonies in North America and the West Indies. The American poet, Longfellow, told the sad story of these exiles in a famous poem, *Evangeline*.

In 1713, France recognized England's ownership of Nova Scotia and also gave up Newfoundland. The contest for the rest of the territory continued. Then, in 1759, a British general, James Wolfe, stormed the Plains of Abraham, a plateau in Quebec City, high above the Saint Lawrence River. The attack was bravely resisted by General Louis Joseph de Montcalm, but in the end the British won. Both generals lost their lives in the fierce battle. The next year, the British took the city of Montreal. New France became Canada. During the American Revolution, Quebec and Montreal were again stormed, this time by American colonists. They held Montreal briefly, but were defeated at Quebec.

The British and the Americans continued the exploration of the Canadian west which the French had started. No exact boundaries had yet been set in this region. The great Columbia River was named for the square-rigged sailing vessel of New Englander Captain Robert Gray, who entered its mouth in 1792. President Thomas Jefferson sent explorers Lewis and Clark to follow up Gray's discovery. In 1807 an English explorer, David Thompson, found the Columbia's source and mapped the entire Columbia River system in Canada as well as in the American northwest. In the 1780's and 90's a Scotch-born Canadian, Alexander Mackenzie, made the first passage across the North American continent, exploring part of the Arctic, edging his way over the Rockies and canoeing down the Mackenzie, Peace and Fraser Rivers.

During this time there were disputes, threats of war, even war itself along the undetermined border between Canada and the United States. In 1812, the United States went to war against England. The Canadians, loyal to their mother country, fought bitter battles with American troops around the Great Lakes. It

wasn't until 1818 that the Great Lakes boundary was agreed upon. In 1838, lumbermen of Maine and New Brunswick came close to starting a war over disputed territory, but in 1842 a treaty settled the matter. In the far west, the United States claimed ownership of the whole Columbia River valley, basing its claim on Captain Gray's early discovery of the river mouth. Canada claimed Oregon on the basis of David Thompson's explorations. In 1846, the two nations traded claims — Canada agreed to stay north of the 49th parallel and the United States to stay south of it. Another bitter argument — about the Alaskan border — wasn't settled until 1903.

Perhaps these disputes helped Canada grow as a nation. British Columbia joined the Canadian confederation on the condition that a transcontinental railway would link her with the eastern provinces. In 1885 the Canadian Pacific Railway was completed. One by one other provinces joined, the last being Newfoundland in 1949.

Today the provinces are also connected by the Canadian National Railway, the Trans-Canada Highway, finished in 1962, and two transcontinental airlines, Air Canada and the Canadian Pacific Airline. Another important link is the huge pipeline which stretches in two directions from Alberta, rich in oil. Through the pipeline oil flows west to the Pacific coast and east to the Great Lakes.

Oil is only one of Canada's treasures. She leads the world in production of nickel and asbestos. She is the second-largest producer of gold, platinum, zinc and cobalt, necessary for making high-speed tools. She is the third-largest source of silver, lead and of molybdenum, needed for steel and spaceships. She is fourth in copper. From the forests which cover more than half the country come lumber and the wood pulp used in newspapers. From the prairie lands comes abundant wheat. Canada has sold hundreds of millions of dollars worth of it to the Soviet Union and the People's Republic of China. They are her biggest wheat customers. Uranium, iron, steel, aluminum, automobiles and fish are other sources of wealth for Canada.

Much of the power needed for Canada's farms and factories

comes from her many roaring rivers. Daring engineers have dammed the rivers and strung transmission lines to carry the captured power hundreds of miles over mountains and through the wilderness to communities that need it.

Canada's lakes and rivers give her so much water that a group called NAWAPA, the North American Water and Power Alliance has proposed to channel some of it into water-short areas of the whole continent. If NAWAPA's plan succeeds, 33 arid states in the U.S.A. and six in Mexico would benefit. Canada would also have available still more water for irrigation, power and transportation. Canadians, however, aren't very enthusiastic about the plan. They think perhaps someday they will need all their water themselves and meanwhile they particularly object to Canadian water being called North American.

This treasure chest which nature has filled to overflowing is one of the most varied places in the world to explore. Let's begin in the Arctic section of the Yukon and the Northwest Territories. Even here, the variety is striking. Mountain ranges cloaked in ice and snow, frozen seas, glaciers and icebergs there are, of course, but you must also be careful of the hot sun and watch out for swarms of mosquitoes, flies and bees! In the Arctic summer, especially in the valley of the Mackenzie River, you can pick cream-colored Arctic roses. But you needn't worry about thorns. They don't grow in the Arctic. And you can wander through fields of flowers or over the tundra, a plain of dwarfed trees that grow only a few inches high, without ever worrying about snakes. There aren't any of those, either.

The Arctic, except for the North Pole, isn't as snowbound as you might think. Boston, Massachusetts, and Denver, Colorado, often have more snow. Arctic winters are cold though, 50 to 60 degrees below zero. The polar bears, walruses and seals don't seem to mind the bitter weather. Of the many animals which live in the Arctic they are best adapted to the cold. Exploring in the Arctic, you would be on the lookout for some of these animals: hares who hide in snowdrifts, foxes and tundra wolves, mice-like lemmings, martens and minks, fat, shaggy musk-oxen, the caribou reindeer which supply meat and clothing for the Eskimos and the Husky dogs which pull their sleds.

Inuvik, the Canadian Arctic's newest city, is a good place to meet the Eskimos, especially in April when they come from far around to a festival in honor of the sun. Those who make their homes in Canada's far north, above the 70th parallel, have lived in unbroken night from November to January. Now in April, the days are longer and they know that from May to July, there will be no night at all. In all northern parts of Canada, winter days are very short and summer days last until after midnight, but only in the Arctic does the sun disappear entirely in certain months and in others shine continuously.

At the sun festival in Inuvik, you might see displays of Eskimo art. The figures of animals, birds and people which Eskimos carve from soapstone have modern, sleek lines and are velvet-smooth to touch. Better save your allowance in advance, though. Eskimo carvings are very expensive.

You would also see Eskimo children playing some of their favorite games. One of these, *naglugatak,* is like jumping on a trampoline, except that the Eskimos jump on a walrus skin. Walrus-skin whips are used in *nuglugaktak,* a game in which a ball made of caribou hide and stuffed with moss is flicked about with a whip.

You would notice that the houses and stores in Inuvik are built on stilts, to keep the buildings off the permafrost. Permafrost is ground that, except for a top layer, stays frozen all year round. The top layer melts in summer and a house built directly on it would sink into mud. In winter, when the top layer freezes again, it expands and bulges up in huge mounds which would break up the foundations of a house. That's the reason for the stilts.

Inuvik is on the great Mackenzie River which, like all Arctic rivers, flows northward into the Arctic sea. Not far from the town and the river, the first three Canadian Arctic oil wells were drilled. In the oil camps, most of the work is done in winter, when tractors can pull the 120-foot-high oil rigs over the ice. The drillers must dig as deep as 10,000 feet into the frozen ground.

Farther north on Great Bear Lake, just south of the Arctic Circle, Canada's first uranium deposits were discovered in 1930 and are now being mined. The biggest uranium mine in the world is in Canada, on Elliott Lake in northern Ontario.

Eskimos are among the Canadians working to extract riches from the earth. Some Eskimos still earn a living by hunting and trapping as their ancestors did, but more and more of them have jobs as miners and drillers. Many drive automobiles instead of dog-sleds, and although they built their church in Inuvik to look like an igloo, and they call it God's igloo, not many of them live in igloos any more. They live in stilt houses with modern conveniences.

Life is changing for almost everyone in the Arctic today. Modern science has shown men how to use to advantage what was once thought to be a wasteland. Atomic submarines glide under the ice-cap at the North Pole and satellites equipped with cameras, radios and tape recorders, orbit over it. The satellites send back to earth information which can warn the continent of enemy attack as well as records which help weathermen predict the world's weather. Some meteorologists and oceanologists live on floating icepacks. From there they map currents, ice formations, even the Arctic sea bottom. Also important in the Arctic is the DEW line, a warning system. DEW stands for Distant Early Warning. The line is made up of 60 radar stations which can detect approaching planes. The stations are operated by Canada and the United States together.

Elsewhere in Canada the United States is cooperating in projects that benefit both countries. The two most important have to do with rivers: the Saint Lawrence and the Columbia. In the 1950's Canada and the United States turned the Saint Lawrence River into the Saint Lawrence Seaway, so called because vessels can now carry cargo all the way from the sea through Quebec and along the northwestern border of New York State to the Great Lakes. Once the river was too shallow for big ships. Seven locks, built by the two countries, made the difference. The locks raise and lower the water level to accommodate ships of all sizes.

In the 1960's the United States and Canada agreed to control another great river — the Columbia. The United States advanced money to pay for three dams on the British Columbia section of the river which will prevent it from flooding in the states of Washington and Oregon. In the flood season the dams store up water which can be drawn on as needed to produce electricity in the United States. Near Libby, Montana, the United States is building a fourth dam, on the Kootenay River, which flows into the Columbia. Canada is helping to pay for the Libby dam. Engineers say that when all the dams are finished in 1973, the electricity produced from the rivers can be sent through power plants and transmission lines as far south as the Mexican border.

At about the same time another great power dam will come into full operation on the Peace River in British Columbia. It will generate more power than any other dam in this hemisphere or in Europe.

An important British Columbia power plant is located on the Kemano River, which empties into a deep inlet of the Pacific Ocean. If you didn't know this plant was there you would never find it. All you can see from the outside are folding metal doors, four times the height of a tall man, set in the slope of a mountain. Inside the mountain are the turbines and generators that produce power. Slung from peak to peak across glacier-filled mountain passes, transmission lines carry the power to an aluminum smelter at Kitimat, 50 miles away. On the opposite side of Canada, 3,000 miles away, is a sister powerhouse, Chute des Passes, also set in a mountain, high above Quebec's Peribonka River. Its power is carried for 200 miles to the world's largest aluminum smelter at Arvida. The company which runs the Arvida and Kitimat smelters, Alcan Aluminum Limited, produces from them 21 percent of the world's aluminum, thanks to the force of Canadian river power.

The Fraser, in British Columbia, is one of Canada's most fabled rivers. Milky gray with silt from glacial streams that feed it, the river loops like a letter *s* through the southern half of the province. The story of the Fraser is one of gold and of men from as far away

as Australia following the lure of the gold. From the coast they struggled up the deep river through the 500 miles of wilderness. They came on horseback and on foot. They fought the Indians, who rolled stones down on them from the cliffs above. Some were massacred, some were drowned, but some survived and built the Cariboo Trail, a 300-mile-long, 18-foot-wide road along the sheer-walled chasms. After the builders came more gold-seekers with pack camels imported from China, lumbering oxen, horses and mules. By 1862 they had dug millions of dollars' worth of gold from the Fraser region.

In the canyon today a new road replaces the old trail and over a new railroad long trains come and go. The gold-rush days are past. Only a few ruined mines and a few old miners remain.

Some day the Fraser may produce new wealth if, like so many of Canada's rivers, it is harnessed for electric power. Right now it is the largest unused source of water power in the whole of North America. The heavy volume (3 trillion cubic feet a year) which it pours into the Pacific Ocean and its long (nearly 1,000 miles) descent from the Rocky Mountains make it an engineer's dream of the perfect river to dam for power. But so far, all the engineers' hopes have been dashed by a fish. Salmon.

Hosts of sockeye, the best salmon for canning, swim up the Fraser to spawn. Canadian and American canneries both want this fish and so — to make its passage upriver easier — a U.S.-Canadian Commission built a fish ladder at Hell's Gate. This is a section of the river so narrowed by landslides during the building of the railroad, that the squeezed current twists like a corkscrew and is forced up into the air like lava from a volcano. In this seething cauldron, hundreds of thousands of fish used to be battered to death. Today's fish ladder, over which the salmon travel safely to calmer waters beyond Hell's Gate, was designed by engineers at the University of Washington. It consists of concrete pipes laid on the river bed and fastened into the sides of the canyon. A series of cross walls inside the pipes create pools, each pool a little higher than the one below. The fish swim up from one pool to another through slots in the walls.

Although it is possible to build fish ladders into dams, canneries in the United States and Canada are afraid that a series of dams on the Fraser would block off too many fish. And so the Fraser goes its own way to the sea.

Before it gets there, it is joined by the Thompson. Unburdened with glacial silt, the Thompson spreads a broad layer of clear blue far across the clay-colored Fraser at their meeting place. Northeast of the junction, along the banks of the Thompson, is British Columbia's dry belt, eroded by winter ice and snow. The wet cold has leached minerals from the cliffs, bringing to the surface stains of violet, red, orange and beige. Ice has carved strange images in the rocks. Some look like animals, some like long-ago kings of Egypt. The people there call these ghostly figures "hoodoos."

The dry belt is hot country in summer — the hottest in all Canada. It's not uncommon for the thermometer to read 110°. Under a sun so fierce it burns your eyes, little grows except spicy-smelling sagebrush. In some spots along the river, however, the people have pumped up water for irrigation, and in those oases Canada's finest tomatoes and potatoes are produced.

South of the Thompson is the Okanagan Lake country, a complete contrast with the desert. Gentle, rolling and green, it is Canada's peach orchard. Here are grown some of the finest peaches in the world.

The northern valleys of the Fraser and Thompson are cowboy

and Indian country. Horses, cows and sheep are raised on ranches that may be as big as 500,000 acres. Among the dashing cowboys at rodeos you would see many fine Indian riders. The farther north you travel the more Indians you meet. Along the roadside, you come across totem poles, tall wooden carvings of animals, birds and people with animal or birdlike faces. The Indians who carved them believed they brought good luck to their families. You see some of the families still living in teepees, others on neat little farms.

Not many Indians own their own farms, however. In British Columbia, as elsewhere in Canada, most Indians are very poor. In 1966 the government set aside $112 million to build decent houses for Indian families, to bring them electricity, roads and sewers, and to help them improve their health. There is so much sickness among them that they can expect to live only half as long as other Canadians.

This north country has few homes. Most of the people of British Columbia live in the south and half of them live in the coastal city of Vancouver, on the Strait of Georgia. Victoria, the capital of the province, is situated across the Strait on a 300-mile-long island also called Vancouver. The Japan current, flowing across the Pacific Ocean from Taiwan, gives the island and the city a mild climate. Watered year-round by heavy rainfall, roses bloom in December. The cities of Victoria and Vancouver are both famous for gardens, not only in public parks but all around everybody's home. In Vancouver, people's bungalows are as gaily colored as their flowers. Often the front steps are painted deep rose red. In Victoria, people live in more stately fashion, their rambling houses and gardens screened from view by high hedges.

Vancouver's fascination is its variety and its international atmosphere. In Vancouver shops you can buy anything from an Australian boomerang to a Chinese kimono. Some 10,000 Chinese have built there the second-largest Chinatown in North America.

The city has two harbors — equally colorful in quite different ways. The inner harbor is Canada's largest port for year-round navigation. Here fishing boats maneuver among ocean liners, dredges, ferries, barges, tugs, and cargo ships from the seven seas. The outer harbor is for fun. Here swimmers, water-skiers, families with picnic baskets, youngsters with small sailing craft, spend many happy weekends.

Where the westernmost tip of the city stretches into the Strait of Georgia, stands Canada's second-largest university, the University of British Columbia. Its campus of almost 1,000 acres reaches back toward the majestic mountains that clasp Vancouver city like a crescent and cover most of the province.

Great peaks, many of them glittering with glaciers, rise also in the western and northern parts of British Columbia's neighbor, the province of Alberta. Prairies stretch across southeastern Alberta

and on and on through Saskatchewan and Manitoba. In a good
summer when there is plenty of rain, the prairies turn to gold —
the gold of wheat. In a bad summer, when there is a drought, or
when swarms of grasshoppers or a disease called rust attacks the
wheat, the prairies turn brown and brittle and the faces of the farmers turn grim. Yet behind the grimness, there is hope. Perhaps next
year's crop will be the best yet, and make up for the losses. Government experimental farms work tirelessly to invent new types of
wheat which rust won't attack and which will ripen before summer drought sets in. The government also helps farmers hire low-
flying planes that spray the wheat to protect it from grasshopper
hordes.

At the same time many prairie farmers are learning not to de-
pend only on wheat for their livelihood. They are also planting less

delicate crops, such as oats and barley, and raising cattle and hogs. During bad years for wheat, farmers can count on these for cash.

They sell the cattle and hogs to meat-packers in Winnipeg, the capital of Manitoba. Winnipeg is also one of the world's largest markets for the sale of grain. A great railroad center, the city is a busy, modern one, crowded with tall office buildings.

All the prairie province capitals are lively. Edmonton, Alberta's capital, is a manufacturing city and the oil refinery center of the country. The province is rich not only in oil, but also in natural gas and coal. Regina, capital of Saskatchewan, grew from an Indian campsite called Pile of Bones. Today it is the training headquarters for the Royal Canadian Mounted Police.

The "Mounties" wear scarlet coats, broad-brimmed Stetson hats, blue breeches and shiny, high, black boots. When Canada was settling its west, the Mountie's job was to keep law and order in the new settlements and especially to put down Indian rebellions. Today there are 4,500 Mounties and their beat is transcontinental. They often travel such great distances that they have been called

"Riders of the Plains." The reputation for daring and bravery which they won in early days is still deserved and to it they have added a reputation for friendliness. They have special responsibilities in the Northwest Territories. To the Eskimos who live there, the Mountie is many things. He is their postmaster, sorting mail and handing out family allowance checks from the government. He registers births and deaths. He takes the census, he enforces fur and game laws, and he is often doctor and nurse, the only comfort when emergencies are sudden and help is air-miles away.

Beyond the prairie provinces with their vast expanses of farmland, is the center of Canada's major industries — the province of Ontario. In the lake region of the north live miners and their families. Some work in the giant uranium mine near Lake Elliott, others in one of the world's largest nickel mines. Still others dig gold and copper from the earth. In the south are steel and paper mills and factories that produce automobiles, airplanes, machinery, rubber and canned goods. Yet just beyond the smoking factories are rich cornfields, tomato and tobacco fields, dairy farms, apple and peach orchards and vineyards, old brick farmhouses and sweeping elms.

Ontario has more than mines and businesses and farms, though. It's also a center of government and education. The capital of all Canada, Ottawa, is in Ontario. Here the Canadian Parliament meets. The provincial capital, Toronto, is the home of Canada's largest university, the University of Toronto.

East of Ontario is Canada's largest — and most old-world province — Quebec. Quebec is like a piece of France in Canada. In the villages some of the old houses look like those in the north of France — made of stone, long and low, with fat chimneys at either end. Others are wooden, with weathered shingles and blue roofs. Against the house leans the woodpile for the big-bellied stove in the kitchen. In winter, when these villages are drifted deep with snow, the warmth of the stove is comforting. At suppertime the narrow streets are empty and white and still. In warm, good-smelling kitchens big families sit around the table spooning up thick pea soup. Outside, in the cold stillness, the church bell rings.

In Quebec country towns the Roman Catholic church is a center of life and the *curé*, priest, a leader of the people. With the church everywhere becoming more modern, he has less authority

now than in the early days, but the church is still a vital part of the life of Quebec. Today in many Quebec schools nuns and priests teach the classes. In many hospitals sisters tend the sick. In some areas monks have opened up the land and taught the farmers how to grow good crops. The first Bishop of Quebec, François Xavier de Laval, founded one of Canada's great universities, Laval University in Quebec City.

Quebec City, the only walled city in North America, has two levels. The upper town is built on a rock rising straight and sheer from the St. Lawrence River. Tier on tier, its towers and turrets, spires and steeples seem to pierce the sky, and lights at night twinkle like a thousand tiny candles on a dark altar.

Along the river bank is the lower town — narrow streets, old houses, churches, chimney pots, cats and dogs and calling children. Between the two towns steep streets twist their way up the cliffs, lined with buildings wedged deep in the rock. Most people who go by foot between the towns today don't climb, however. They use the handy escalator.

The business streets, in the upper town, are as modern as in any city, but in one old square *calèches,* black horse-drawn carriages with high white wheels, wait for fares. The clop-clop of horses' hooves on cobblestones and the silver chime of church bells are sounds of Quebec City that visitors always remember.

Quebec's — and Canada's — largest city is Montreal, which will be the site of the 1967 World's Fair. The city is built around a mountain on a green island in the middle of the St. Lawrence River. Although 1,000 miles from the ocean, Montreal is a seaport, one of Canada's most important. Oceangoing vessels, naval craft, icebreakers, freighters, river, lake and coastal carriers and small, strong tugs fill the air with their sea smells and hooting sounds of work. Among the shipyards loom large grain elevators and cold-storage warehouses for furs, freshwater fish and other goods from all Canada.

Into the Saint Lawrence pour many rivers and streams from the lakes of central Quebec. The Saguenay, long ago a highway for the canoes of fur trappers and Indians, is the best-known of these. Today eight dams for the production of electric power have been built on the upper reaches of the Saguenay River system. Along the lower Saguenay, however, you can still follow the route of the trappers and Indians in small pleasure boats. You glide between tremendous bluffs that loom far out into the river, cutting it into long, curling inlets. The two most majestic bluffs are called Trinity and Eternity. Listen as your boat veers between them and the captain sounds the whistle. The sound echoes and re-echoes with an eerie wail. So tiny below the black crags along the shoreline, your vessel suddenly seems a fragile thing. You realize how lonely the early explorers of this wilderness must often have been.

A thousand feet above, on Cape Trinity, a small white statue of he Virgin Mary smiles down at you. At least she looks small from the water. Actually she is 25 feet tall and weighs 7,000 pounds!

Her name is Notre Dame de Saguenay and the Saguenayans will be pleased to tell you her story. Nearly 100 years ago, Charles-Napoléon Robîtaille, a trader from Quebec City, was driving his horse and wagon, loaded with goods, across the frozen river. The ice gave way. He prayed for rescue, and somehow his horse pulled the wagon to safety. Robîtaille, however, fell very ill from exposure to the icy water. Again he prayed, asking that he might live long enough to bring up his children. His prayer was answered, though doctors had given up hope for his life. In gratitude, he vowed to put a statue of the Virgin Mary on Cape Trinity.

He found a young sculptor, Louis Jobin, who had worked with wood ever since he was old enough to whittle. It was vital for the statue to be made of light material like wood, for it had to be lifted 1,000 feet up the cliff. Jobin carved the figure in sections, which were floated ashore from a boat onto a tiny beach at the bottom of Trinity. Hardy climbers scaled the cliff. A hand winch was anchored top and bottom and the statue sections were hauled up, assembled, coated with lead to protect them from the weather and painted white. Robîtaille lived for 18 years, until his children were grown.

Across the Saint Lawrence River from the point where the Saguenay empties into it is the Gaspé Peninsula. The northern coast of the Gaspé is a land of steep cliffs, a wild and ragged coastline, where gannets and gulls dive for food, and houses with little vegetable plots cling precariously, just out of reach of the sea.

The southern coast on the Baie de Chaleur — which means Bay of Warmth — is much more gentle. Here the meadows turn white with daisies in July. In the interior are mountains covered with thick forests and hollowed with copper mines.

In the fishing villages along the Gaspé coastline, cod is king. On almost every beach, nets are spread to dry and in every harbor tall-masted fishing boats rock with the waves. The fishermen are friendly folk, and you could easily get an invitation to "put for out," as they say, with one of them. He would tell you that his boat is built according to a design which the original French settlers brought with them in the 1600's. Only nowadays he has added a diesel motor. The people of the Gaspé are prospering from copper and lumber and, in the summer months, from busloads of tourists. All three industries bring good incomes to Gaspésiens who work for them.

Nevertheless, the people keep some of their old folk arts. You can buy beautifully handwoven woolen skirts and scarves, with silver and gilt threads, table linens brightly dyed with berries from the woods, and wonderful woodcarving. Along one of the Gaspé's steep, straight-up and straight-down roads, a little boy might hail you with a model of a schooner in each hand. He has made the models himself, with their delicate bark sails and matchstick spars. He sells them for very little and he will probably also be glad to give you his address and become your pen pal. It you can write in French, so much the better.

Across the Baie de Chaleur from the Gaspé are three of the Atlantic provinces: Nova Scotia, New Brunswick and Prince Edward Island. Many of the people who live there — fishermen, lumbermen, pulp mill workers, potato and fruit farmers — have to struggle for their living. On the average, they earn 25 percent less than people in the other provinces. Every year some 20,000 of them migrate to other parts of the country, seeking better jobs. The three provincial governments have formed a council to try to create more jobs by starting more industries. They hope by 1970 to offer 18,000 new jobs each year.

Nova Scotia, with its Scottish festivals held to the tune of bag-
pipes, its rocky capes where red-roofed lighthouses send their beams
across a lashing sea, its high, forested hills and great inland lakes, is
the most dramatic of the Atlantic provinces.

Northern Nova Scotia is a rugged island, Cape Breton. On its eastern coast stand the ruins of an old fort, Louisburg, built by the French. For a time, before the English conquered the island, French pirates lived in the fort and sallied out from it to attack fishermen from New England who had sailed their vessels to the Grand Banks off the coast of nearby Newfoundland. It's often foggy at Louisburg and wandering through the ruins it's easy to imagine you see ghosts of that old pirate colony in the wreaths of fog slinking along the ramparts.

48

It's also easy to imagine why Alexander Graham Bell, inventor of the telephone, loved Cape Breton so much that he asked to be buried there, near his summer home outside the town of Baddeck. His grave is at the summit of Beinn Breagh, Gaelic for Beautiful Mountain. From this quiet spot you can see the full circle of the horizon. Below you, at sunset, the lakes of the Bras d'Or — arms of gold — gleam like the precious metal which is their namesake.

Mainland Nova Scotia, in the south, is gentle and rolling. Here, in Annapolis Valley, apple trees blossom pink and white for eighty

49

miles in late May. Little fishing villages nestle in deep coves that are often dotted with islands. The round islands with their crowns of fir trees look like birthday cakes with green candles.

Halifax, the capital, has so many long coves leading in from its great harbor that it seems as though the sea were poking its fingers all through the city. At long piers thrust far out into the harbor, all kinds of ships have docked — sometimes pirate ships and smugglers and battleships, and today, as always, the ships of traders and fishermen.

Across the Bay of Fundy from Nova Scotia lies New Brunswick. Its capital is Fredericton, but its principal city is Saint John, ancient and dignified, also a cheerful, bustling, international deep-sea port and a busy industrial center. Here sugar from the West Indies is refined. Tea, coffee, and spices are unloaded from the holds of foreign ships, packaged and sent out again to fill grocery shelves across Canada. Fish is processed in huge quantities, many cans of cod and salmon ending up in America's supermarkets. Logs are beaten into pulp for paper and raw cotton is woven into textiles.

Another New Brunswick city, Moncton, sits at the top of the estuary, or long, narrow mouth, of the Petitcodiac River, which flows into the Bay of Fundy. In the Bay, the tides are so strong, rising as high as 26 feet, that they force water up the estuary in a tall, rapidly rolling wave like a tidal wave. This inrush of water is called a bore. The Fundy bore is one of seven in the world.

An arm of the Bay of Fundy, Passamaquoddy Bay, reaches into Maine. The United States and Canada hope to dam the bore and use Passamaquoddy to store the dammed-up water. The stored water will be released as needed to turn electricity-generating turbines in power houses to be built in the United States. The electric power will be used by the New England states and Canada.

Imagine a mill with wheels turned by the moon! This is what will happen when the "Quoddy" project, as it is nicknamed, is complete, for the tides it harnesses are controlled by the moon. There is only one other such tidal power plant in the world, in northern France on the Gulf of Saint-Malo. Another is planned by the Soviet Union on its Arctic seacoast.

North of the Bay of Fundy, and separated from it by a land bridge which connects Nova Scotia with New Brunswick is the Gulf of Saint Lawrence. Tiny Prince Edward Island lies in the Gulf between the two provinces. Sometimes called the "Garden of the Gulf," it is mild in climate and rich in loamy soil. Potatoes, oats, barley, fruit and cattle farms stretch from one tip to the other, creeping close around its capital, Charlottetown. Tourists flock to the island to enjoy the sandy beaches of its north shore, explore the low, red sandstone cliffs of its southern shore and visit the farms where silver foxes are bred. When the island is joined to the mainland by a causeway by 1970, still more visitors will vacation there.

Northeast of Prince Edward Island is Canada's newest province,

Newfoundland. Until the middle of this century at least half of all Newfoundlanders earned their living cod-fishing off the Grand Banks. Fishing is still important and so is seal-hunting, an annual spring event on the icefields which cover the northern part of the province. Since Newfoundland joined Canada, however, and since

World War II, when army bases brought new ways to the island, there have been changes. Once an army airfield, Gander, in eastern Newfoundland, is today one of the world's largest international airports. Thriving towns have developed on the rocky, wind-whipped coasts and a pulp and paper industry has made use of the woodlands which cover the interior. Coal, lead, copper, zinc and iron are also being mined there.

Many of the largest towns, like Saint John's, the capital, are crowded on the Avalon peninsula at the island's southeast corner. Others are along the eastern coast. These sections are warmed by the Gulf Stream, whereas the western coast is chilled by the Labrador Current. Where the warm and cold currents meet at the Grand Banks, fog blankets the sea and fishermen must sail warily, tooting their horns as they weigh anchor.

Labrador, the mainland section of Newfoundland, lies across the Strait of Belle Isle. Except in the area around Grand Falls at the headwaters of the Hamilton River and a series of lakes from which the river flows, the people of Labrador are mostly Eskimos and wandering Indian tribes, There are not many of them. Lack of transportation is the reason for the scanty population. Labrador is almost roadless and too mountainous for airfields.

In the lake region the story is different. Here is one of the world's richest deposits of iron and at Grand Falls a great water power development. A railroad connects the region with the city of Sept Îles, on the Saint Lawrence River in Quebec. Sept Îles' huge steel mills are supplied with iron from the lake region and run by power from Grand Falls.

Now that you have seen something of all Canada's provinces and territories, do you have a favorite? If you made friends with a Canadian boy or girl your age and asked that question, the answer would almost certainly be the section where your friend lives, for a Canadian is apt to be particularly attached to his own part of the country. That is, if your friend is a "settled" child. Likely as not, he isn't. Today, many children move all over the country, traveling with their engineer fathers from mine to mine, or dam to dam, as Canada continues to open up its treasure chest of natural resources. If you asked a child in an engineering family where he had come from, he wouldn't name a town. Instead he might say he came from Arrow dam on the Columbia River or the Denison uranium mine in Ontario, or wherever his father had worked last.

A child's life in the wilderness is a happy one. You would enjoy visiting a construction camp family. You would be surprised to find a most uncamplike community of attractive prefab houses, well furnished and equipped with the same household helps, like washing machines and driers, that you probably have in your home.

There's a fine playground for children and a recreation club for grownups. In the winter, there's wonderful sledding, skiing, snow-shoeing, skating, ice hockey and curling. Ice hockey and curling are favorite Canadian games. In curling, a Scottish game, the play-

ers heave heavy stones with iron handles across the ice, much as a bowling ball is heaved along an alley. In the summer, there's swimming in a nearby lake, or perhaps in a community pool. There may be motorboat and canoe trips.

Except around Vancouver, Canadian winters are so long and the summers so short that the people sometimes describe their climate as "ten months winter and two months poor sleighing." However, though Canadian summers may be cool in the east, in the west and on the prairies they can be scorching hot.

Much of the fun at a dam or mine site is outdoors. Children often keep horses among their many pets. It's exciting to ride over narrow trails through dog-haired timber, as people call the thick hemlock forests. Sometimes the children pretend they are the first explorers of Canada and keep a sharp lookout for Indians. If they ride high enough into the mountains they may find snowbridges — hollowed-out, iced-over drifts that never melt.

Boys like to go hunting and fishing with their fathers. With luck they may catch salmon, trout or oolichans for supper. Oolichans are sea smelt that swim upriver to spawn. The children may spot a sea lion, something like a seal, chasing the oolichans. Or they may help their father bring home a deer. In the distance, they may see nimble mountain goats, bighorn wild sheep, moose, foxes, martens and lynx. They try to avoid the cougars and the bears, which sometimes visit the camp at night. Garbage pails have to be anchored down and the lids locked on or the bears would have the garbage scattered all over the camp by dawn.

The cougar is a savage animal that preys on sheep and sometimes attacks people too. The engraving of him on the new Canadian quarter makes him look more harmless than he really is. On 50-cent pieces, dimes, nickels and pennies you can see mackerel, rabbits, wolves and doves. The lucky child with a silver dollar has a coin with a wild goose on it. The government is issuing these animal coins in 1967 in honor of the 100th anniversary of the Canadian confederation. Canadians use the same money system as we do.

In a construction camp, families may spend a good deal at the small supermarket that's usually on the site. The outdoor air makes everyone hungry and mothers must be good cooks. These families enjoy the same foods that are favorites with all Canadians. Besides fresh fish and game from nearby woods and streams, there are smoked cod, haddock and salmon and perhaps frozen shrimp, a tiny, curled-up variety from the Pacific coast. In summer there are fresh vegetables from their own gardens and peaches and blueberries trucked in. There is tangy cider in the fall, stacks of pancakes for winter breakfasts and all year round a creamy Canadian cheddar cheese that melts on your tongue like peanut butter.

Sundays, families go to church, either on the campsite or in town if town isn't too far away. Big construction camps usually have their own schools and church services. Most families are likely to belong to the Roman Catholic, Anglican or Presbyterian churches, or to the United Church of Canada. These are Canada's biggest church groups.

Weekdays, children in a camp school study the same subjects as other Canadian youngsters. Their courses are much the same as yours, but they are expected to work much harder at them than you do. Most children start learning to read and write in kindergarten, where they go when they are five. Often they have already spent a year or two in nursery school. At six they enter first grade. After the sixth grade they may go to junior high school, then on to three years of high school, or they may stay in elementary school until the eighth grade and take four years of high school.

There are three different kinds of high schools. One kind prepares students for a university; another prepares them for a trade. The third kind, the "composite" high school, offers separate courses for students planning to go to a university and those planning to learn trades. Some high schools have five-year courses; students who graduate from these can finish their university training in three years instead of the usual four.

Students must pay at universities, but schools are free and attendance is required until a child is 14 or 16, depending on the province where he lives. The schools are run by the provinces, just as our schools are run by our states. But it's a lot harder for children to switch schools from one province to another than it would be for you to change schools between states. In Canada the courses and textbooks differ a great deal from province to province and children of traveling engineering families often have a lot of trouble with switchovers. The national government is trying to persuade the provinces to make school programs more alike.

In a campsite classroom, in a big city school, or in one of the little one-room schoolhouses that can still be found in remote parts of the country, Canadian children, while working hard, are eager for vacation time. Canadians love their out-of-doors and on weekends and vacations many of them think nothing of driving vast distances over bumpy dirt roads to reach mountain, lake and riverside lodges on a Friday evening. In the back of the car, there may be a chicken in a pot, freshly stewed with vegetables and ready for supper on arrival. "How much longer, Dad?" the children ask, their mouths watering as the car speeds into the wilderness.

Canada, you see, is still uncrowded even though it is a very modern nation. The cry of a loon across a lonely lake is as much a sound of Canada as the shriek of a steel mill whistle at Sept Îles. Canadian boys and girls have the good fortune to live in a land where there is room for everybody and where tomorrow will be even greater than today.

SOME IMPORTANT DATES IN CANADIAN HISTORY

1000 — Leif Ericson probably landed.

1497 — John Cabot discovered Newfoundland.

1534 — Jacques Cartier explored Gaspé waters and discovered the Saint Lawrence River.

1608 — Champlain founded first settlement at Quebec; subsequently explored the Saint Lawrence, Great Lakes and northeastern United States.

1663 — Canada, then called "New France," became a French colony.

1670 — Hudson's Bay Company organized by the British.

1710 — British attacked Acadia, took it and renamed it Nova Scotia. Acadians exiled.

1713 — French recognized British ownership of both Acadia and Newfoundland.

1759 — Contest for Canada between French and British culminated in the Battle of the Plains of Abraham, which the British won. The peace treaty gave Canada to the British.

1775 — Americans from the thirteen colonies during the revolution unsuccessfully attacked Quebec and Montreal.

1780–1807 — Period of exploration of the west. Mouth of Columbia River discovered by Captain Robert Gray, a New Englander; its source discovered and its entire system mapped by David Thompson, an Englishman. Alexander Mackenzie explored the Mackenzie, Peace and Fraser Rivers.

1812 — Canada and U.S. engaged in battles around the Great Lakes.

1818 — Great Lakes Boundary lines agreed upon.

1838–1842 — Lumbermen of Maine and New Brunswick contested boundary line; dispute settled by treaty.

1846 — Canada and the U.S. agreed to boundary line in the far west.

1867 — British North America Act authorized uniting of Canadian Provinces. Nova Scotia, Quebec, Prince Edward Island and New Brunswick established a confederation.

1870 — Manitoba joined confederation.

1885 — Canadian Pacific Railway completed.

1873 — British Columbia joined confederation.

1905 — Boundary with Alaska settled. Saskatchewan and Alberta joined confederation.

1931 — Canada became an independent member of the British Commonwealth.

1945 — Canada became a founding member of the United Nations.

1949 — Canada joined North Atlantic Treaty Organization. Newfoundland joined Canadian confederation.

1959 — Saint Lawrence Seaway opened.

1962 — Trans-Canada Highway completed.

1964 — Canada and U.S. signed a treaty for joint development of the Columbia River.

1967 — World's Fair held in Montreal on 100th anniversary of birth of united Canada.

Present: Canada continues to develop her tremendous storehouse of natural resources, maintains an open immigration policy which provides labor for the development; attempts to strengthen the national government and to improve living conditions for poorer citizens.

HOW TO PRONOUNCE FOREIGN WORDS IN THIS BOOK*

Word	Pronunciation	Word	Pronunciation
Acá nada	ah-*kah nah*-dah	Inuvik	*In*-nu-vik
Baie de Chaleur	*Bay*-ee de *Shall*-er	Jacques Cartier	Szhahk *Car*-tee-ay
Beinn Breagh	Ben Bray	Jolliet	*Jo*-lee-*et*
calèches	kal-*esh*	Kanata	*Kah*-nah-tah
Chute des Passes	Shyout day pass		
coureurs des bois	kur-*er* de bwah	Louis Jobin	*Loo*-ee *Zshoh*-bahn
curé	*kur*-ay	Louis Joseph	*Loo*-ee Szhoh-*sef* de
Charles-Napoleon	Sharl	de Montcalm	*Mont*-calm
Robîtaille	Nah-*poh*-lay-ahn		
	Roh-bee-teye	Marquette	Mar-*ket*
François Xavier	*France*-war	naglugatak	*nah*-loo-gah-*tak*
de Laval	*Zay*-vee-ay de	Notre Dame	No-trah Dahm de
	Lah-*vahl*	de Saguenay	*Sah*-gwen-ay
		nuglugaktak	*nug*-loo-gak-*tak*
Gaspé	Gas-*pay*		
		Sept Îsles	*Set*-eel

* Italics indicate accent. Where there are no italics, the stress is equal.

Index

THE GETTING TO KNOW BOOKS
COVER TODAY'S WORLD

Africa

GETTING TO KNOW AFRICA'S FRENCH COMMUNITY
GETTING TO KNOW ALGERIA
GETTING TO KNOW THE CONGO RIVER
GETTING TO KNOW EGYPT
GETTING TO KNOW KENYA
GETTING TO KNOW LIBERIA
GETTING TO KNOW NIGERIA
GETTING TO KNOW THE SAHARA
GETTING TO KNOW SOUTH AFRICA
GETTING TO KNOW RHODESIA,
    ZAMBIA AND MALAWI
GETTING TO KNOW TANZANIA

Arctic

GETTING TO KNOW THE ARCTIC

Asia

GETTING TO KNOW BURMA
GETTING TO KNOW THE CENTRAL HIMALAYAS
GETTING TO KNOW HONG KONG
GETTING TO KNOW INDIA
GETTING TO KNOW JAPAN
GETTING TO KNOW THE NORTHERN HIMALAYAS
GETTING TO KNOW PAKISTAN
GETTING TO KNOW THE RIVER GANGES
GETTING TO KNOW THAILAND
GETTING TO KNOW THE TWO CHINAS
GETTING TO KNOW THE TWO KOREAS
GETTING TO KNOW THE TWO VIETNAMS

Caribbean and Central America

GETTING TO KNOW THE BRITISH WEST INDIES
GETTING TO KNOW COSTA RICA, EL SALVADOR
    AND NICARAGUA
GETTING TO KNOW CUBA
GETTING TO KNOW GUATEMALA
    AND THE TWO HONDURAS
GETTING TO KNOW MEXICO
GETTING TO KNOW PANAMA
GETTING TO KNOW PUERTO RICO
GETTING TO KNOW THE VIRGIN ISLANDS

Europe; East and West

GETTING TO KNOW EASTERN EUROPE
GETTING TO KNOW ENGLAND, SCOTLAND, IRELAND
    AND WALES
GETTING TO KNOW FRANCE
GETTING TO KNOW GREECE
GETTING TO KNOW ITALY

GETTING TO KNOW POLAND
GETTING TO KNOW SCANDINAVIA
GETTING TO KNOW SPAIN
GETTING TO KNOW SWITZERLAND
GETTING TO KNOW THE SOVIET UNION
GETTING TO KNOW THE TWO GERMANYS

Middle East

GETTING TO KNOW IRAN-IRAQ
GETTING TO KNOW ISRAEL
GETTING TO KNOW LEBANON
GETTING TO KNOW SAUDI ARABIA
GETTING TO KNOW THE TIGRIS
    AND EUPHRATES RIVERS
GETTING TO KNOW TURKEY

North America

GETTING TO KNOW ALASKA
GETTING TO KNOW AMERICAN INDIANS TODAY
GETTING TO KNOW CANADA
GETTING TO KNOW THE MISSISSIPPI RIVER
GETTING TO KNOW THE U.S.A.

Pacific

GETTING TO KNOW AUSTRALIA
GETTING TO KNOW HAWAII
GETTING TO KNOW INDONESIA
GETTING TO KNOW MALAYSIA AND SINGAPORE
GETTING TO KNOW THE PHILIPPINES
GETTING TO KNOW THE SOUTH PACIFIC

South America

GETTING TO KNOW ARGENTINA
GETTING TO KNOW BRAZIL
GETTING TO KNOW CHILE
GETTING TO KNOW COLOMBIA
GETTING TO KNOW PERU
GETTING TO KNOW THE RIVER AMAZON
GETTING TO KNOW VENEZUELA

United Nations Agencies

GETTING TO KNOW F.A.O.
GETTING TO KNOW
    THE HUMAN RIGHTS COMMISSION
GETTING TO KNOW UNESCO
GETTING TO KNOW UNICEF
GETTING TO KNOW THE UNITED NATIONS
    PEACE FORCES
GETTING TO KNOW W H O
GETTING TO KNOW WMO

A MARI USQUE AD MARE